Mindful thoughts for
FATHERS

First published in the UK and North America in 2020 by

Leaping Hare Press

An imprint of The Quarto Group
The Old Brewery, 6 Blundell Street
London N7 9BH, United Kingdom
T (0)20 7700 6700
www.QuartoKnows.com

British Library Cataloguing-in-Publication Data
A catalogue record for this book is available from the British Library

ISBN: 978-1-78240-955-7

This book was conceived, designed and produced by

Leaping Hare Press

58 West Street, Brighton BN1 2RA, UK

Publisher: *David Breuer*
Editorial Director: *Tom Kitch*
Art Director: *James Lawrence*
Commissioning Editor: *Monica Perdoni*
Project Editor: *Niamh Jones*
Illustrator: *Lehel Kovacs*

Printed in China

1 3 5 7 9 10 8 6 4 2

MIX
Paper from
responsible sources
FSC
www.fsc.org
FSC® C008047

Mindful thoughts for
FATHERS

A journey of loving-kindness

Ady Griffiths

Leaping Hare Press

Contents

New
Beginnings

This book is a journey of loving awareness: of your body, your thoughts, your feelings, your children, and the people and world around you.

Pause for a moment as you read this and become conscious of where you are. Notice what you see and hear, the sensations in your body, the movement of your breath, the thoughts passing through your brain. Mindfulness can be as simple as that – though of course, there is more to learn. And that learning is worth doing: it can help you develop parenting skills by creating self-awareness and increasing your energy, positivity, empathy and compassion from moment to moment.

While this is a spiritual and emotional exercise, it is also very practical and real. Fatherhood involves earning money, shopping, preparing food, cleaning dishes, laundry, wiping bums, soothing toddler tantrums or teenage frustrations, helping with homework, and much more. With practice, we can become mindful during the pleasures and the pains, rejoice in the joys and address the difficult times with a deep acceptance.

In traditional Buddhism, the purpose of life is to turn your heart and mind towards awakening, to become an enlightened human being full of mindfulness, love, courage and wisdom. This might seem like a tall order for a dad. However, our everyday actions can actually help us be in touch with this vision of life. Fatherhood is full of many highs, lows and plateaus: an epic adventure through the beautiful landscape of life with people we love the most, and for whom we would do anything. But sometimes we may find ourselves feeling alone in the deep dark valleys, lost, confused or scared, wondering how we found ourselves there in the first place, and how to find our way back onto the pathway of our old 'normal life' again. We can learn to recognize and embrace these changes instead of letting them overwhelm us.

Mindfulness can act as a compass to help you navigate your way through these moments, and reflect on who you are and why you are here, letting you find your own way to a purposeful, valuable and generous life. Raising sons or daughters is an intimate and deeply personal experience that makes you face both the best and the worst in yourself: you can't hide from anything, unless you want it to come back and bite you like a naughty child that you haven't given your loving attention to. Mindful fatherhood is a practice which helps you to turn towards everyone and everything you do with care and kindness. It is a journey that will open you up to every experience you have as you guide your child through the world. You don't need to waste time not enjoying yourself. Being, witnessing and contributing to the life of a human being are precious gifts, and you can learn to love your own life as a father.

Precious
Human Birth

I can remember being at the hospital to see the first baby scan of my daughter, watching the pulsing rhythm of her little heartbeat and the wriggling of her hands and feet. The immediate sense of the preciousness, seeing this little human being alive within my partner from an act of lovemaking only months earlier, seemed completely miraculous.

I immediately felt a deeper bond with this being. Everything somehow became real, and I know many fathers have experienced similar amazing moments. The reality of your child's imminent arrival seems to set in at this point because you can see the moving image, as well as feeling the movements in the mother's body in the later stages of pregnancy. It is these precious moments when we feel truly connected to our new little family that we hold in our memories and hearts forever.

LIFE CORDS

During pregnancy the baby and mother are linked by a physical life cord, and when our child was born I somehow felt vividly and imaginatively more connected by an imaginary life cord to my whole family – mother, father, sister, nephews, uncles and aunts, cousins, grandparents – and the whole of humanity. Somehow we are all sharing this journey together, linked by the breath of life, as well as everyday struggles, pleasures and pains. We will always be connected to one another, making our way in and out of each other's lives and sharing experiences and the world that we co-habit together. Our time on Earth may be short, but we can learn to live in the present and savour every moment mindfully, with awareness and open-heartedness towards those around us and our children.

Part of what makes this life so important is that we know it may go at any time. When we really understand that deeply, it's easier to commit to enjoying being alive together on this amazing planet. Our lives are precious and fleeting, but can be rich and full of joyful moments. Enjoying your child play happily, or sharing laughter with them will give you these rewarding memories to treasure.

A famous poem by the fourteenth century Tibetan master Tsongkhapa called 'Precious Human Birth' speaks of how life is uncertain and ephemeral, like a beautiful raindrop that appears and disappears almost in an instant. This is an understanding that can be a huge help with parenthood. There is a birth; a new being appears; it moves towards maturity; then eventually leaves. Time is short, and must be treasured; it's a powerful thought which can help you to commit yourself to your highest intentions. Everything in life is impermanent, and seen clearly, can be beautiful. In this way, we can enjoy every moment with our children, no matter how brief that moment may be.

HOLDING FOR THE FIRST TIME

I remember being handed my child; somehow she was miraculously breathing by herself, covered in blood yet still beautiful, and I was amazed, enchanted and in love. It was a relief that she had survived her passageway into life: it hadn't been an easy birth for my partner, a very long labour of love, as many are – and the rest of life, from birth onwards, becomes a blend of labour and love.

If you have been around a lot of babies, you will know that they are all different, and this somehow makes them all the more wonderful: we are all unique from birth to death. Every experience that they have, and that you have alongside them, will be unique and wonderful in its own way. Nobody will experience exactly the same childhood or fatherhood; even if you have twins or triplets, your experiences with each of them will be totally different and equally special. Knowing this can help you value the experiences you have with your children as individuals, and accepting that they change constantly adds value to every minute spent with them.

Every moment you can remember to be mindful is valuable; every moment you look at your child with loving awareness can re-invigorate you when life is hard. The softness and vitality in their eyes, their breath and motion, their very selfhood, is ever-changing, now and throughout their lives.

Somehow, who your child is now and who they may become is like a seed that will hopefully grow and flourish as your nurturing awareness shines on them like the warm glow of the sun's rays. As they hopefully become fully mature human beings, we will also have to let go of more and more as time passes. But for now, in the moment, we can enjoy their glorious presence and the imaginary life cord between them and us, and perhaps begin to imagine who they will become in our family tree.

First Phases of
Fatherhood

The early phases of fatherhood bring unique challenges. If you haven't been around a newborn baby before then it can be full of surprises, but this is something that we can also enjoy mindfully.

If you witnessed the birth of your child you are likely to have seen a very different view of the mother of your child, at least if you've never seen her in labour before. If you were in hospital, there will have been unfamiliar sights and sounds, such as strange medical equipment, people and processes, as well as concerns for the mother and child: is she ok? Is the baby ok? These are all normal thoughts and feelings for a very intense time of heightened attention.

The birth process contains primal surprises for many fathers: the mother's body has dramatically changed; the life-giving umbilical cord and placenta have a bit of a bizarre appearance; often the baby doesn't look exactly how we imagined. Who is this alien-looking life form coming out of the mother anyway?

Do you remember what you saw, heard, thought or felt? Was any of it startling? I remember, for instance, being struck that I had to literally hold my baby's head up. The reality seemed very strange to me: here I was holding an example of the most highly developed species on the planet, and she couldn't support herself, or even see properly. And why didn't I know it would be like that before?

The journey home from hospital, the uncertainty of whether the child seat was in the car correctly, and the sudden awareness that this little being's entire existence was in our hands opened up a kind of primal fear and sensitivity to her life, and the people around us. Suddenly, as parents, we related to the rest of life in a different way.

THE FIRST FEW
DAYS OF UNCERTAINTY

These first days can go in a few directions and we will never be able to predict them beforehand. The mother may have had an easy labour (if there is such a thing) or a very difficult and traumatic process that no man can completely understand. At this stage, fatherhood is very different from motherhood. For instance, no matter how much you use your imagination, you will never be able to recreate the unique experience of giving birth or breastfeeding a baby.

Your ability to connect and empathize with the mother of your child, and offer the relevant physical, emotional and mental support at this stage, creates the possibility of a strong foundational basis for your own fatherhood journey. Part of being a good father to your child means being a good partner to his or her mother – or, if the two of you are not together romantically, still offering the mother all the help, support and respect you possibly can.

NEW DAYS ARE DAWNING

The reality of the baby's arrival – the feeding, winding, soothing, holding, walking, washing, changing nappies, sleeping, not sleeping, and repeating over and over – has begun. Days turn to nights and nights turn to days, and sometimes one feels like the other. During the night, tasks can feel more difficult as you may be half asleep, or at least wishing you were.

Some parents are blessed with babies who sleep all the way through the night, while others have babies who wake every hour. If you had or have one of the latter, you will know the experience of being wide awake when it seems like the rest of the world is asleep. Our little one awoke a few times most nights in early phases, and sometimes the only thing that I could do to help her get back to sleep at night was movement, so I would walk with her tucked up cosily in a sling, feeling a mixture of frustration at not being able to have my full night's sleep, fluctuating to a warm, fuzzy love and appreciation of this little person. Walking round and around your kitchen and seeing lights on in other houses, and other people being awake, eased the sense of feeling alone: there were thousands of other people having a similar experience throughout the world. Reflecting can help you feel connected, part of one big human family going through life phases that are akin to your own.

Foundations of
Mindful
Fathering

Mindfulness provides us with a strong foundation: it is a home base to return to inside yourself when you need to find resources for everyday parenting challenges. For this reason, it can be helpful to understand its core foundations as a practice.

The original Indian Pali word for mindfulness, *sati*, has multiple meanings, often translated as 'to remember', 'to recollect', 'to bear in mind', or 'to apply attention to an object of concentration'. The recollection and remembering do not necessarily mean to think of the past; they can also refer to being present in the moment (a daily responsibility for fathers). We are creating moments of recollection, of remembering to be aware throughout our day, pausing to give attention to how we are, who we are with, where we are and what is important to give our attention to now in the present.

PRACTICE MAKES PERFECT

Training our mind to recollect is similar to training a muscle to perform an activity: if we repeat it enough times, it becomes natural and easy for us to do, but if we don't practise, it remains difficult or becomes even harder. It can therefore help to try to create specific regular times to practise and create mindfulness. This can vary depending on your current lifestyle; it might be at the beginning, middle or end of your day. It can be as simple as sitting or standing still, sensing your body, feeling the breathing, being aware of sights or sounds around you, the thoughts you are experiencing and feelings within you for a few minutes, or a more full practice of meditation.

MEDITATION CREATES MINDFULNESS

Meditation is a specific practice for creating mindfulness, allowing us to have the moments of recollection that we may need in our daily life as fathers. The *Ānāpānasati* meditation (often translated as 'mindfulness of breathing') is a practice where we apply attention to the physical sensations of breathing, to create focus and calm amidst a broad awareness of our body, mind and feelings.

There are many different versions of this practice. A simple version is counting each exhalation until you reach ten, then beginning a new cycle afresh. You can choose a period of time that suits you, a few minutes, ten, fifteen or more if you like. If you have a baby or young child this can be challenging, so do what you can, wherever you can.

It sounds simple, and in some ways it is, but it isn't always easy: on some days it will come naturally, and on others, your mind will wander before you reach a count of three. If you are stressed, busy or emotionally distracted your mind may wander around to many other things.

That is normal, so try not to worry: it becomes more familiar and sometimes gets a little easier with practice. Remember to treat yourself kindly: try not to tell yourself 'I can't do this', even if it's difficult. Gentleness and forgiveness are, after all, fine qualities for a father to cultivate, and remembering to be kind to ourselves is something that we, and those around us, can benefit from.

THE FOUR FOUNDATIONS OF MINDFULNESS

Traditionally, in Buddhism the four foundations of mindfulness are taught to create calm, clarity and insight as a method. The idea is that by being aware of direct experience instead of getting carried away with stories, views and opinions about life that may bear little resemblance to reality, we free ourselves from suffering.

The four foundations are simply described as mindfulness of the body (*kayā*), the sensations or feelings (*vedanā*), thoughts or mental states and events (*citta*), and phenomena (*dhammās*).

Using these to know ourselves, we can develop a flexible responsive mind to move between different mind and body states and aspects of reality – which is a very positive foundation for fathering. It enables you to create focus on the young person in front of you and give them the attention they need, and to be aware in an expansive way of the situation they are in, where and how they are, and the emotional landscape they are navigating. This can be applied to parenting children of all ages, from baby to toddler, young child to teenager, and by setting such an example, we can also help our children grow up as aware, balanced and responsive human beings. Gradually, they can learn to be aware of the foundations themselves in their own everyday actions, passing on the skills of mindfulness to the people that they meet along their journey.

Changes
of
Identity

Who am I? It is a question we can continually ask ourselves. Some come up with different answers every time, while others see themselves as having a static identity that magically stands still through the eternal flow of time.

In reality though, you are always changing: your identity can never be a single fixed thing, and you can be many characters with different aspects which come alive in different situations. Fatherhood itself is not a single role, but a combination of many.

People perceive you in their own ways: how you are with your family is different to how you are with old friends from school, or people you study or work with, but there will be qualities of character that continue and run through you like rivers in a landscape, shaping who you are in all contexts. It is these we tend to think of as our 'self'.

THE ONLY CONSTANT IS CHANGE

We are always changing, even while we keep trying to create a permanent identity by identifying with our relationship, job, passions and interests. Realistically, though, when we examine ourselves clearly, we can see that we are one continual process of transformation.

Prior to becoming a father, you may have had certain ideas of who you were, what you liked and were capable of, and perhaps you imagined how your life as a parent would be. The expectations of taking your child to the park every sunny afternoon, teaching them about the world you're sending them into and showing them off to your friends and family may be somewhat shattered when faced with the realities of parenthood. Taking a step back from these natural desires and evaluating them may feel difficult in the face of the everyday humdrum, and this is only to be expected.

You will probably not have the same amount of time and energy to invest in the interests and passions you had before being a parent, which can be frustrating and feel like a loss. Acknowledging that, and finding ways of managing how you think and feel about that loss (and when the time is right also starting to organize yourself to allow for some of these things to return) can help you navigate through that process. Don't worry: the state of being tired and busy with a young child is just as impermanent as everything else.

WHO AM I NOW?

Good question! Once you become a father you will never be the same person again: something deep within you will have changed. You can't deny the existence of your child, and that awareness creates an ethical responsibility which you will be aware of for life. How you behave in response is entirely up to you and will be influenced by many conditioning factors in your own life, including your own family upbringing and the cultures around you.

So, who are you now? How do you accept who you are now? Can you look for and find aspects of your new life which you appreciate and enjoy as much as the interests and activities you did before? This can take time to establish, but with practice it will happen.

Transformation isn't easy: butterflies have to make a lot of unseen effort within the cocoon before they are ready to emerge and fly. Make space for care and kindness to yourself, as well as those around you as you make the transition into being a father.

WHERE ARE THE INSTRUCTIONS?

As many new parents will tell you, it would be great if children came with an instruction manual. Sadly, though, that is simply not possible: every child and relationship between father and child is unique and in constant flux. The same is true when it comes to your relationship to the mother of your child: she too will be continually changing, and you will grow together and apart at different times. Sometimes the changes in each other lead to separations, and other times to more closeness, deeper understanding and love.

Mindfulness helps you keep conscious of the reality that, whoever you are now, there is always possibility for new understanding, new experiences, new senses of self. Fatherhood doesn't come with a guide book, but your own awareness can be your best guide.

Internal
Sat Nav

Men are often considered (by some) to be rational
beings who like to know, to understand the whys, hows,
whens and wheres on a conceptual level, who think
clearly and act decisively. And there is nothing like
a baby, with his or her lack of coordination, inability
to communicate clearly, and ever-vulnerable health, to
throw that rationality out of the window. Not-knowing
can be a painful, frustrating process, but can also serve
as a reminder of that fundamental truth of life: we
cannot possibly know, understand or control it all.

Having to know it all is an unfair expectation to put
upon yourself, or anyone else. You, your son or daughter,
and their mother will always find new challenges, new

situations where you have to make a decision you've never faced before. It's time to let go of the expectation that a 'real man' always knows what to do: you don't, and you can't, because nobody could.

LIVING IN THE UNKNOWN

Learning how to be at peace with the unknown is a key life skill as a father, and will take a lifetime of practice. It requires courage to stay present and aware with what's happening to you, or a human being close to you, even when feeling uncomfortable; you have to find your intention to act with care and kindness if you want your child to be safe and happy.

Trusting your awareness, and any life experience you have previously developed in your life, is a good base, especially when mixed with the knowledge that you can always ask others for help. You may also develop your ability to listen to your own internal voice: your instinct and intuition can become a helpful internal compass. It is sometimes difficult to distinguish between intuition and false imaginings; it can be tricky to balance the two extremes of being over-cautious and over-risky. The best thing to do is stay as responsive as you can in the moment, so you don't become the prisoner of habit.

Many fathers will be able to tell tales of how they had to act spontaneously, instinctively, to prevent their child harming themselves or others seriously. Perhaps you have had to make difficult choices to guide you and your family through challenging emotional terrain. I certainly have made a few choices that, while they have worked out all right in the end, could have gone another way.

INTERNAL SAT NAV

One day, driving from teaching on a retreat in Spain, I set the sat nav to avoid a series of long curvy roads – or so I thought. However, at a critical point I misunderstood a direction and went off course, onto a single track bumpy road, down a mountainside, with deep drops to one side and overhanging rocks on the other side, some of which had previously fallen down onto the road.

My partner and I had a few intense conversations about going back (a longer journey), or to carry on without knowing the road. Looking at the visual evidence ahead, it was hard to trust the path ahead would be okay. I quietened my mind down by focusing on my breathing, turned on a song we all liked, and we began singing; this took us from a fearful state of mind into a joyful one. I asked if we were okay to carry on, and we then decided to take a risk and trust my intuition: even though there was fear within us, it did not dominate our experience and we could be bigger than the fear and trust our ability to deal with it.

Thankfully, no rocks fell, and our car didn't skid down over the side. We drove through the worst part, breathed a big sigh of relief, and then the road was fairly simple with a few bumps. I had never been so glad to see paved road before. The moral of my story could be a few different ones – 'Don't trust a sat nav', 'Listen to your partner', or 'Listen to your intuition', (or even 'Take risks in life-threatening circumstances', which is definitely not what I am advising!) – but the biggest take-away for me was that, by gently managing your awareness, you can make sure that whatever decision you take, it will be one that you are later more willing to stand by.

Gift of
Attention

As a parent, you are likely to have felt heart-lifting, wonderful moments when you look at your young child and feel full of awe and wonder. Giving loving attention, the quality of tender yet focused interest, is a natural thing for us to do: we have created this human and are looking after him or her – and yet it is not always easy, and doesn't always come to us spontaneously the moment we become fathers. Sometimes it is good to recognize that it is actually a practice, a process of mind and body training, to fully give our loving attention to a human being.

The quality of looking at and listening to someone with warm, positive emotional intention can feel very different to looking at someone like an object, and both you and the other person can feel that difference. In a colder way of looking, your body will generally feel harder and more contracted and your eyes become narrow, while loving attention opens your eyes and relaxes your muscles.

GIVING ATTENTION

When you are with your child, practise pausing and giving them your wholehearted attention. Start with a foundation of mindfulness of yourself – your body, thoughts and feelings – and then broaden out your awareness to your son or daughter, looking at them with loving eyes and listening to them with loving ears.

This can be easiest when you are very close to them. Perhaps, when giving them a hug, feel the physical contact and connection and look at what you find beautiful and enjoyable in your child: their physical features, their eyes, hair or smile. This can feel like a gift to you and them.

CURIOSITY AND WONDER

Watch them doing something fairly simple, like walking or pottering around by themselves. Try and be curious and interested in them and their actions; see if you can enjoy what they are doing every day. This often creates a 'sympathetic joy' in us as we make their experience a secondary delight in us. I often find wonder arises quite easily as I watch this unique being discover the world and create their relationship with it.

REWARDS OF RECEPTIVITY

We receive rewards from giving attention: a real relationship with your child and a deeper sense of yourself. Of course, this is not always comfortable or pleasant; when your child does something you don't like, try to pause, expand your awareness to include where you are, and take a few breaths to experience the situation with more perspective. That way, this more unwelcome gift can become a welcome one. If we can understand what triggered their behaviour, then we can learn to be receptive to that as well as to the favourable gifts. Thus we can gain self-knowledge and awareness as we create a capacity to be with less comfortable aspects of fatherhood.

ABSENCE AND PRESENCE

We all know what it feels like to be absent in body, heart and mind. For example, suppose your child is trying to attract your attention, and you are half-listening while paying more attention to a message on your phone or thinking about a current concern. Then you realize you actually didn't hear the last words they said.

Giving our attention can be a difficult thing to do when there are so many calls on our time in modern life, but the more we practise it, the better our relationship with our child and ourselves is likely to be. There is no need to beat yourself up: you can just notice when you are not wholly present, and kindly guide your mind back to the moment by looking towards your child and listening to them so they really know you are with them.

Children may like receiving presents from us, but in the long run they enjoy receiving our presence of body, heart and mind even more. It may not give such an intense high as a sugar-coated sweet or be as colourful as a plastic toy, but they know the deep value of love when they receive it, and you will both know when it is missing. A heart that keeps giving love is a heart that keeps love alive, and it is love that our children want most.

Wheel
of Life

Life has a habit of rolling on, like an out-of control-
wheel rolling with us trapped inside it, and it can feel
particularly like that in the busyness of parenting. Life
cycles everyone through various states of being, from
waking up in the morning to going to bed at night,
and we are all involved in the cycle of birth, life, growth,
decay, illness and death. This includes our beloved
children and family.

One aspect most of us don't want to see or experience
is the reality of illness. However, if we recognize that
we all get ill, and allow ourselves to acknowledge this
and be open to feeling the pain and discomfort of being
the sick person or seeing a loved one ail, it can help us

develop the very real and honest quality of compassion. This quality goes a long way, and can allow us to become more proactive and focused when illness occurs, so that we are able to support and help our loved ones through the hardship to the best of our ability.

This is how to transform the suffering into a substantial life experience. It doesn't take the pain away, but it does create a real sense of being with other people and connecting to them even more. If we don't acknowledge the discomforts of life, we cannot live honestly: we are just trying to hide from a real aspect of existence that we share with every other living human being.

Being present with compassion is what our children need from us, whether for minor bumps and bruises, cuts and grazes, coughs and colds, or for more serious conditions. Fathers who are there with the plasters and creams, medicines and supportive arms, guidance and advocacy, are holding their children in their loving attention, and that is what sons and daughters need more than anything.

THE COURAGE OF BEING PRESENT

Being alongside family members when they are ill or suffering can be challenging, yet it can bring out the best in us as we go beyond our own desire for the comfortable and just do what needs to be done. Supporting the return of health and wellbeing, or loving unconditionally when a child has a difficulty that will never really go away, is a substantial gift that will affect you both deeply.

There may be nothing we can do to take away the pain or physical suffering, but we may be able to give a tender quality of looking, listening and holding them in the heart of our attention so they know they are not alone, they are seen and heard and held with love. Sometimes our presence alone can enable some relief and release from the emotional or psychological strain, and allow them a deeper sense of being able to be at ease with discomfort and pain, or at least show that you are there through thick and thin. Holding our children when they are crying, upset or miserable with a cold or stomach bug, or when there is nothing that can be done other than give comfort, love, food and drink, helps them feel that, even at rock bottom, there is support and love to rest upon.

LIGHT IN THE DARKNESS

I know when I've visited hospitals with my daughter when she has had an asthma attack, there is a kind of steely resolve that arises to just do whatever needs to be done to get her there to receive the medicine she needs. Even if it's the middle of the night and I am tired and don't want to be there, something deep inside can motivate me to let go of my self-based desires for comfort and provide what is needed in the moment. And I doubt there is a parent alive who hasn't done something similar, and gone beyond themselves because of the deep, caring connection to their child's life. You can probably remember moments when you have gone out of your way to help, to get the medicine, give them the necessary liquids, or to hold them or your loved ones through the night, to be their beacon of light in the darkness.

When seeing or receiving support from others, we can take a moment to practise appreciation and gratitude for their efforts, whether they are family members or people in caring professions. They create the conditions for life to keep rolling on wherever possible, and it can be easy to take these people for granted. Pausing to show that you recognize their efforts will go a long way to alleviating any sense of isolation you may be experiencing. None of us can go it alone in sickness; we need love to support us through illness towards health and wellbeing. We cannot hide from illness on the wheel of life; we have to keep on rolling with as much love, care and awareness as we can.

Chop Wood,
Carry Daughter

There is an old Zen phrase which has been translated as, 'Before enlightenment, chop wood, carry water; after enlightenment, chop wood, carry water.' Its meaning has been contemplated for centuries.

One aspect is the message that before we become fully awakened, wise and compassionate, we can train ourselves by doing simple things, repeatedly, with as much mindfulness as we can – and over many years, we can refine our awareness. This repetition of simple activities with mindfulness over a long duration of time is sometimes referred to as the gradual approach to enlightenment. Yet also within the Zen traditions it is often said that awakening can happen suddenly at any time, and we may have many moments of mini-awakenings along the way until we become more fully awakened. Even if we don't get there, perhaps we can enjoy the journey mindfully.

These mini-awakenings can arise amidst the most mundane daily work, perhaps because we can be more wholeheartedly mindful when we are not caught up in overthinking. When we are doing simple tasks, we are in a good position to train ourselves to be here, now. There is an element of present moment awareness when we are not focused on gaining something or reaching an end, such as trying to become 'someone special', or even become 'enlightened'. Sometimes the most enlightened thing you can do is be mindful at whatever you happen to be doing. There are many tasks that offer such opportunities, but in the early stages of fatherhood, the two key jobs of food preparation and transportation stand out as good examples of everyday tasks that assist in creating wellbeing and keeping your family moving and connected to the world.

FOOD PREPARATION

Even the preparation of bottled milk for babies, has to be done with awareness: if milk is too hot it will burn the baby's mouth, but if it's too cold the milk may not mix well or the baby may not like the temperature – babies can be quite picky, as you may know!

This daily repetition of a simple 'chore' can be mind-numbingly boring or an opportunity to become more subtly aware of what we are doing, seeing this moment afresh. Often it is the thoughts about what we are doing – such as 'I don't like this', or 'I can't believe I have to do this again' – that create a blockage to a happy experience. So we can practise being aware of how we hold the bottle, our posture, the work of our hands, trying to appreciate the pleasure in doing a task with care, and using it as a mini mindfulness meditation.

As your newborn grows into a child and you give more time to preparing real meals (even if you're just heating up frozen food when you're tired), you can still use these moments to gather wholehearted attention and awareness of these everyday tasks as acts of love for your little being. We can also start to help them become interested in food preparation and cooking, learning to provide food for themselves as they become ready to do so. These are actions infused with intention and a wish for them to be well, healthy and happy.

CARRY DAUGHTER

I have fond memories of carrying my daughter as a baby in her sling. Transporting our children is one of the practical ways fathers can participate physically: we may not be endowed with the right bodily parts to produce nutrients for our baby, but we can certainly carry them lovingly, supporting their body so they can feel at ease – whether their particular nervous system settles when being held still, or from the regular rhythm of walking, cycling or being pushed in a pram.

Transporting babies and children is often a familiar task for men, and we may like pram-pushing as an opportunity to walk mindfully. If you prefer gentle exercise, you can be aware of placing your foot down in every step, or you may be more athletic and use the time to catch up on running in a mindful way: I have seen whole families running, taking turns to push a pram. Either way, there is the discipline of being aware of the needs of your child, whether they are awake and lively or dozing in peace.

Other times, we are juggling trying to hold the baby, fold the pram and somehow cram it into the car, bus, train or plane, and the best we can do is try to pause and create calm and clarity. Child-ferrying isn't always relaxing, but with mindfulness we can respond to the need in hand, so that no matter what, we transport our child in a loving way.

Skilful
Habits

Creating and maintaining positivity requires effort, and it's not always possible to be positive. Accepting that fact is actually a realistic place to start: unless you are some kind of superhero dad from another planet, it's highly unlikely that you will always be chilled out and cheerful.

A plastic smile helps no one: good attitudes and healthy thinking can't be created on a superficial level. What we need is to find ways to be in touch with the good, the bad and the difficult. Everyone feels the temptation to get lost in fantasies about how life could or should be, but lasting happiness needs to be built on mindfulness of body, mind and feelings and a sturdy relationship with reality.

THE FOUR SKILFUL EFFORTS

There are some useful teachings from the Buddha known as the 'four right efforts' or 'four skilful efforts'. I will use the latter term here, as 'right' can sound rather black and white: this is about developing skills, and there are many ways to find a 'right' solution to a problem.

So, what are these skilful efforts? They come in two pairs: preventing and eradicating unhelpful states of mind, and developing and maintaining helpful ones.

Unskilful states of mind are characterized by greed, where we only care how to satisfy our own desires; hatred, where we act harshly to anyone or anything that thwarts those desires; and delusion, where we forget that our desires are not the only thing in the world that matters – even to us.

SKILFUL FATHERHOOD

As fathers, we need to accept these unhelpful states of mind will arise within us. We may want to do something nice for ourselves, and our child wants or needs the exact opposite. If we let our frustration drive us to speak or act harshly as a result, though, it's not going to do us, or our child, any favours. All we will do is model bad behaviours for our child to mirror back to us – or else hit us in later years with a therapy bill! It's easy to let unskilful states of mind overwhelm us, but they aren't a recipe for anyone's happiness and it's good to notice when they bubble up inside ourselves.

Skilful states of mind, on the other hand, are characterized by generosity, love and wisdom. When our child is doing something we don't like and we are able to empathize, understand, and see why they are behaving as they are, then we're in a much better place to give what they really need. Putting aside our own needs and wants takes generosity, but it's generous to ourselves as well as our son or daughter: responding kindly (though that may sometimes, of course, mean a kindly 'no'), means they will feel more content. As every father knows, a content child is a better-behaved child, and a better-behaved child means a more contented dad.

Be alert to unskilful states of mind building up in yourself. Look out for angry, harsh thoughts; feel the heat in your belly, chest or head; notice a habitual action, such as wagging a finger. Then stop. Bring your awareness back to your body; create a stable upright position. Take a few deep breaths. You know this is not how you want to act, so create a mindful moment, calm yourself, and find your better intentions.

Choosing skilful states of mind is a creative act, helping you to nurture a family where everyone's sense of playfulness is free to expand. What activities do you and your kids enjoy that help you change your moods and thoughts? Dancing, messing about and laughing release energy and create joy; acrobatic balancing and pairing up in gymnastic movements create supportive connections; and slow, careful games like chess encourage patience and attention. Make these part of your lives together, and bring your loving attention to bear while you and your children enjoy them together. You may find you grow and mature almost as much as they do.

SURFING THE EMOTIONAL SEAS

Think of your state of mind as a living ocean, with your current actions surfing along the top. When you're in a good mood, you can ride the waves of previous skilful actions – but you can't just drift. You will need to keep making subtle efforts to stay balanced, or the next wave may knock you back into deep water.

Creating skilful habits is deeply positive, both for you and for those around you. If you are in a resourceful state, you can help lift the mood of others and make a playful day or a united learning experience, which will help you feel happy about your parenting efforts.

Loving You,
Loving Your Family

Learning to love yourself completely can take time. You may have a good regard for who you are and find it relatively easy to be kind in your thoughts and words, but more than likely, you have good days and bad days and your sense of self fluctuates depending on what's going on in your life.

Our own thoughts and feelings can help or hurt us, but they can be subtle and it can require a gentle persistence to be aware of them. Creating a continuity of self-care helps to keep alive our intention to act with care and kindness towards ourselves.

UNLIMITED KINDNESS

There is a beautiful meditation practice, called '*mettā bhāvanā*' in the original Pali, which can be translated as the 'cultivation of loving kindness', or 'development of unlimited friendliness'. This can have remarkable positive effects on you, your loved ones and the people you meet in daily life, particularly if practised regularly.

Like other meditations I refer to, there are different versions, and you can choose the duration depending on the time you have available. I'll describe a straightforward one here, but by all means do more research if this is something that speaks to you.

Begin by being aware of how you are, and try to create a warm glow of positive intention of love and appreciation within yourself. Think of it like starting a small fire to warm yourself up, and then try to create a brighter, larger fire to radiate outwards to other people. One method can be to begin by repeating phrases in your mind like, 'May I be well, may I be happy, may I be at peace'. This first stage can create an openness to the idea and intention.

The second stage is to imagine a good friend, or someone that brings a smile to your face. Try and see, hear or have a sense of them, as though you are with them. You can also repeat the phrases in relation to them – 'May you be well, may you be happy, may you be at peace' – and see how your imagination responds. Or, perhaps, imagine them enjoying something they love doing, like playing happily with their child or family, or doing an activity they love. Feel that sense of joy and fondness in contemplating them.

In the third stage, we start to spread that well-wishing intention outwards to people we may recognize but don't know so well, perhaps other parents or teachers from school. Then radiate that goodwill out towards other people: other children and families, people that live near you, and ultimately people throughout the globe. You can include the whole life cycle of humans from newborn babies, to toddlers, school children, teenagers, adults and elders. Wish them to be well, happy and be at peace.

There can be many beneficial results if you make a habit of this meditation. You may find yourself being more emotionally open and friendly towards people you don't know, or being able to sustain positive states of mind more easily and for longer. The regard for your own and other people's wellbeing and happiness is a precursor for many nurturing states of mind.

CARE AND EMPATHY

Some other qualities that Buddhism particularly values are *mudita* (sympathetic joy), *karuna* (compassion), and *upekkha* (equanimity). All are precious resources for parenthood: they allow you to rejoice in your kids, forge good relationships with other families, support your children in vulnerable moments and keep your head amidst the everyday ups and downs of fathering. They help develop a broad range of emotional responsiveness and empathic skills so we can care for others as much as ourselves, ultimately leading to a happier state of mind for us and an active kindness that changes people's lives.

GRATITUDE

Another method for creating a foundation of positivity and loving awareness can be practising gratitude. Reflect on, and bring appreciation to, whatever you can feel grateful for today. It needn't be complicated; it could be the air you are breathing, the food you ate today, the clothes you have on. Or even that you are able to have time to read this book now to help yourself, or the presence of your loved ones in your life that made you feel like reading it. Perhaps the thoughts to give you a lift right now are the little things your child did recently which made you smile, or an appreciation of your parents, who gave you life itself.

Feeling appreciation and gratitude, recreating the imaginative connection between us all and recognizing that we are all intimately connected to each other can help us feel fully alive and can allow us to appreciate the beauty of our existence.

Being
'Good Enough'

Every father creates their own journey: making it up as they go along, influenced by their own experience of being fathered well, or not so well, perhaps reading information online or in books, and hopefully supported in their own development by other fathers.

In some circles, it is rare for fatherhood to be spoken about. The contribution fathers make to their children can be seen as secondary to mothers, and in some cases, and the early stages in particular, it can be – but to view it completely in that way diminishes our role and responsibility. It may be important for you to feel the rewards of contributing in a significant way to your child's journey to adulthood, in which they will hopefully become someone capable of being effective in the world in a way that makes a positive difference to those around them. As we know, children need a lot of time, energy and love invested in them every day. This takes confidence and conviction from us, a feat which isn't always easy.

DOUBT AND WISDOM

The process of fathering can be challenging: self-doubts, fears and comparisons arise along the way like thorny bushes tearing at you and your self-view. You will probably have your own thoughts that you say to yourself, like, 'That's not the right way', or 'You're not a good father', 'That dad does it better than me', or 'I wish I was a better dad'.

Being mindful of these thoughts and examining them to see if they are helpful or harmful, and thinking clearly to face your inner demons of self-doubt and fear, will help you cut through the wilderness with wisdom, revealing a clear pathway for you and your child to confidently walk along together.

BEHAVIOURS

It can be hard to acknowledge and own up to our own difficult behavioural traits. I used to think of myself as being fairly calm and patient, but in the early phases of fatherhood, with all its new unfamiliar tasks and the struggle of keeping up with work whilst sleep deprived, I realized my patience was easily worn down. Like everything else, our ability to be calm is based on conditions like being able to have enough food, rest and sleep. Thankfully, the practices of mindfulness and loving kindness can help you re-centre yourself to recapture your sanity more quickly when you lose your cool – and let's be honest, there probably aren't many people alive who don't lose their cool at least sometimes.

I like a particular story about Morihei Ueshiba, the founder of aikido – a martial art based around the ability to be calm and focused. The story goes that a student asked him, 'How do you manage to be centred all the time?' The master replied, 'I don't; it's just that I re-centre myself so quickly that you don't notice when I am off balance.' What matters is not staying calm every single second of our lives, but how quickly we come back to being calm, and being kind when we have not been as patient as we would wish to be.

PERFECTIONISM

Many of us carry an unconscious idea of what a good father would be like which only reveals itself when we do something that doesn't match up with this perfect behaviour, and start criticizing ourselves with harsh thoughts. Perhaps it's more helpful to focus on what's good enough. We won't and don't have to be perfect: our children can still grow up healthy and well adapted if we make some mistakes along the way.

Find ways to think more kindly, and catch yourself when you are telling yourself off. Ask yourself, 'Did I harm anyone?' If you did, then okay, you can be aware of that, apologize, and set an intention to act differently next time. Ask yourself too: are the hard thoughts you're inflicting on yourself proportional?

You might be hurting yourself more than your original mistake hurt anyone. It can be hard to walk the line between being honest with yourself in a heartful or a hurtful way. Here it is good to strike a balance to allow your behaviour to change, rather than falling prey to the two extremes of letting yourself off the hook or being overly hard on yourself.

There is always room for improvement, but being able to look back at how we have parented our child, it could suffice to be able to say it was good enough. Yes, we helped create them and assist them in becoming who they are, but there is a certain point when we must accept that no matter what we have given them, they will need to form their own way and build their own life. A father who puts his heart into parenting and does his best is as much as anyone could hope to get, and most of us do fine on that.

Life Lessons
We Need to Learn?

As a father, you will probably have realized there are many unfinished lessons you need to learn. Every man has areas they need to improve upon or develop. These may be about the ways of the world; we can call this 'outer' knowledge, about how to survive, be emotionally engaged and help provide for our family. Alternatively, there is the 'inner' world of self-knowledge, where we can develop ourselves in deeper, broader, more emotionally expansive or subtle spiritual ways, or perhaps begin to unlearn previous conditioning so that we can be more open and receptive to more aspects of ourselves, life or people around us.

OUTER KNOWLEDGE

The world doesn't stand still, and neither does our understanding of it: education and knowledge are constantly being refined. Often, you will find that your child is learning things at school, college or the university of life that show your own previous learning is now out of date. If you treat this as an opportunity to refresh your understanding, it can keep your relationship with your child fresh: give them your interest, and share their passions, and you can feed their thirst for knowledge, learning and development. If you show real respect for their minds, few things will motivate them more than feeling like they're teaching Dad a trick or two.

This is a time to be open to the unknown. There are always going to be new methods of learning and sharing information. Who knows what the future will develop into? So use your mindfulness to help you be curious rather than conservative, and take advantage of that. There are modern museums, performances or ancient sites you and your family can visit, creating treasured moments together; you can be outdoors in nature, observing the wonders of the sky and solar system with the naked eye or through observatories; you can immerse yourself in new ways of appreciating the vast and complex universe. Children often love learning and understanding; support that, and you can bond with them and enliven your own mind at the same time.

INNER KNOWLEDGE

Turning the lens inwards to review our inner world is just as fascinating as the external world. We can discover hidden caves of the heart and mind that need work, a process similar to mining for hidden treasures and refining the raw materials we find there to make them more beautiful. Each of us has latent qualities that can be polished to shine. The process will vary: maybe you need more gentleness, softness and openness, or maybe more directness and firm focus.

Mindfulness is how you stay sensitive to these needs so you can make the wisest choices about what kind of polishing your personal qualities most need.

INNER AND OUTER WORLDS

Awareness of both inner and outer experience requires you to be aware, reflective and creative. In reality, both are endless realms to explore and learn about: as long as we are alive there is always the possibility of discovering something new. This may sound like a tall order, but at heart, it's quite simple: stay open-minded and never assume you know all there is to know about the world, yourself or your family. All may yet surprise you; that's what makes life such fun.

QUALITIES AND REFLECTIONS

Reflecting on what qualities we still need to learn can bring focus. Somehow, bringing a child into the world and enabling them to grow up has a kind of mirroring effect: it shows us the things we still need to learn and improve upon. These could be about becoming more responsible and mature, for instance in personal care-taking or looking after finances, or the opposite: learning to hold life more lightly, making sure it's not all about work and duty, and creating more time for relating to other human beings. You will have your own unique lessons, and so will other dads.

There is something particular about family life when you are trying to live consciously: it shows you your own quirks in ways that are hard to avoid. Every little habitual use of words or phrases, physical gestures or actions, can become magnified as your child reflects it back – or as they grow older, they comment on your behaviour, challenge it, or, even worse, laugh at you and who you have become. Don't panic: you probably did the same to your own parents. Take it as a lesson, mindfully reflect on whether it's time to take your kids' advice (even if it isn't exactly sugar-coated) or time to exercise some compassion for their still-immature understanding, and keep loving them and yourself.

Playtime, Playgrounds & Pathways

Playful parenting is an excellent way of exploring mindfulness and expressing loving awareness to children. We all know that play is key to a child's development as they learn about what they are able to do, physically and psychologically. They expand their range of movement and use their imagination to create endless scenarios, and in this way they develop courage and confidence for future life. Watching or joining with a child in play is also something adults can enjoy, but unfortunately many of us lose the ability to play as we grow up. Becoming parents is a chance to rekindle it.

NO EQUIPMENT NEEDED

Designated spaces like parks and playgrounds are, of course, wonderful, and swings and slides, sports grounds and courts, can be magnificent training for your child to explore their physical and mental capacity. From the discipline of sport to the careless freedom of a swing, these are the places that are designed and built to be enjoyed by us. But these physical tools aren't essential in the process of having fun, because using your imagination, and encouraging children to activate theirs, makes playtime possible anywhere, from long train or car journeys to seemingly boring places like banks, supermarkets and hospital waiting rooms. Instead of allowing ourselves to become bored in an outwardly tedious situation with our child, we can take time to notice their restlessness, pause, and see it as a great opportunity for imagination, growth and excitement with just the simple use of our own minds. No equipment needed. It can make the difference between a dull day and a fun one.

THE IMAGINATIVE MIND

Playing around, being different characters with my child and her friends, is one of my favourite things as a father. We can be magicians, wizards, warriors, comedians, dancers, scientists, cowboys and cowgirls, astronauts or hundreds of other roles in short spaces of time. Doing this means keeping ourselves open and flexible, changing our body language, or voices, our states of mind – the very same openness to change that mindfulness teaches. Be ridiculous: create laughter out of nowhere. Playfulness means letting yourself go, stepping outside of your 'adult' role and freeing yourself to take risks. It's liberating for you and for the child or children involved.

Imaginative play is also a good opportunity to create healthy boundaries and better communicate with your child. By giving them your full attention and by distracting both of your minds with some harmless fun, you may find communication becoming easier between you both. Exploring likes, dislikes, troubles, worries and

fears through play and reflecting on them together
is a meditative way to connect with your little ones.
Teaching them about the world in a less formal setting
than school will allow you to approach topics mindfully
with loving kindness, and lets them feel your good
intentions as you give them useful advice.

There's nothing stupid about joyful silliness. Be the
tickle monster, the evil pirate, the crazy scientist. You
aren't making a fool of yourself: you're teaching your
children the courage and confidence to find their voices
and express themselves, to collaborate with others,
to create complex relationships with people and with
themselves. They also find ways to create their own
identities, learning about who and what they like.

THE SECURE SELF

Our experiences shape our minds, right down to creating
new neural networks within the brain: exploring fun
healthily in childhood is the foundation for a good
adulthood. In later years, your children may be more

difficult to reach; teenagers don't look to their parents quite so much. But many return to these parks and playgrounds to hang out with friends at night. The mindful love you gave them when they played as little ones will still be shaping their instincts even as they become more independent.

Making time for play and being playful as a family can make you feel more flexible, open and responsive to your child. Laughter is the best medicine, and by lightening a difficult time with some healthy fun, we can allow our children to develop more healthy responses to the difficulties they might face later in life.

Daily life is challenging for everyone, so de-stress together and play with your sense of self. If you can fool around, you can laugh about the more serious sides of life. Go on: take some time out to play today.

Being in
Nature

Nature can be profoundly life-affirming, enhancing our creativity and freedom. It also has its dangerous, destructive side: every parent knows we need to provide careful guidance to ensure our child stays as safe as possible in nature, and doesn't stray too close to a rocky ledge, swim too far out to sea, or put their hand too close to a campfire.

As fathers, we need to balance the roles of risk-taker and caretaker, walking the fine line between expanding borders and encouraging adventure, and setting safe boundaries so our children learn to respect nature. There are so many life skills that we can help our children to learn if we take the right approach to the great outdoors.

Even if we live in cities and urban areas, we can introduce them to the awesome power of the natural elements with whatever form of nature is present around us. No matter where we are, there is always at least one or two of these elements present and they have different qualities to explore and enjoy wholeheartedly.

EARTH

Children often love playing with earth in its various forms: sand, earth, stones. Shaping different structures and watching them fall down, or breaking them down on purpose (or having them broken down by siblings) are formative experiences for many. Depending on what natural expression of earth you have near to you, there will be an opportunity for play nearby, whether it's making sandcastles on the beach or collecting pebbles in the park. Earth can also be combined with other elements like water to create fantastical structures like castles, palaces, dens. Mindfully enjoy the solidity, the potential to make something tangible.

WATER

Whether you're jumping up and down in puddles, splashing around in rivers, watching a still, calm lake, or learning to swim or surf in the sea, there can be something ecstatic about being in water, especially for children. Mindfulness is a good companion here because it can help you enjoy the moment and forget the usual parental fussing: yes, your kids may be getting wet or muddy, but does it matter in this moment? Not compared to the joy they're feeling. You can make a mindful exercise of sorting out their soaked clothes later; just for now, let their delight be the inspiration for yours.

FIRE

Warming our hands near a blaze after a cold walk, or telling stories and toasting bread and marshmallows over a campfire, can remind us of our primal nature. Life without fire would be very different for humans. Of course we need to teach children to be careful and respect the potential dangers, but don't let that be the only lesson you provide. Setting things up safely and responsibly creates a free space to enjoy the awe and wonder of watching sparks of light rise towards the sky, playing with sparklers or nourishing yourself from an outdoor barbecue. Mindfulness teaches us to be in the moment in an ever-changing world, and what changes faster than a flame? Fire relies on air to be alive and we rely on warmth and air to be alive; be present with that.

AIR

Nature can move us physically and emotionally, and there are few better ways to experience that than enjoying how the air can buffet us about. Go out in wild winds and let yourselves be blown about and holding your jackets out like parachutes; fly kites and watch them soar high in the sky; try windsurfing and feel the air drive you across the water; watch the air flows catch the sparks from your fire and send swirling smoke into the sky. This is nature acting directly upon you.

FINDING YOUR PLACE

Think about what natural scenes you have the best access to. Maybe you have city parks, or perhaps there are rivers, woods, forests, hills or mountains with caves to explore together regularly or if you go on holiday. Finding enjoyable ways of being in nature is a way of being mindful together, and will create memories that become a lifelong gift. When our awareness is absorbed by our contact with the world, we feel fully alive in body and mind and in direct contact with life itself. In this open and awake state of mind, we can connect even more to our children, enhancing the joy that we experience as a parent, even if it's just on the walk to school or a weekend trip to the park.

Holidays
&
Hell-days

Holidays with children can be delightful or difficult (or both!). You can need the patience of a saint, which sometimes you will have and sometimes you won't – after all, you are only human. We can invest a lot of desire and expectation in holidays, and often visualize them as being a certain way. When we create all the right conditions, both internal and external, it can be great. However, we often have to face the clash of our desires with the reality of what happens.

That happens all the time in life, of course, but holidays can amplify the frustration because of the extra desire and expectations we attach to them. Mindfulness can be a sanity-saver here, turning the stress into an opportunity for insight into the way we think and feel about life. You can learn a lot from noticing what you want to happen and how you want to feel, even if things don't quite work out that way.

FACING THE FRUSTRATION

When your fantasy aligns with reality, it's easy to feel very positive. When it doesn't, though, you have two options: get more frustrated at the painful difference between your desires and reality, or examine it with mindfulness. We can ask ourselves questions like: what was it we wanted? What were we looking for? Was it a specific feeling? Could the specific event we were wishing for have given us that feeling? Then gradually, as we start to understand what we wanted, we can move towards acceptance of what is happening now.

In some cases we can create that desired feeling in where we are and what's happening now, even if it is different to the imagined version. For instance: maybe you were hoping for a sunny day so you could enjoy a restful day on the beach while the kids played in the surf, but it's raining, so you are stuck inside with seemingly nowhere to go because all the local activities require good weather. How can you be more at peace or happy with the reality in front of you? Can you pick up an umbrella and dance down the road singing in the rain, then have a warm bath and hot drink afterwards instead? Create a game, story, dance, play together? What could a creative possibility be?

You may not be able to accept the difference immediately; it might take time and effort to try a few things and see what works. But transformation is often possible. I remember a childhood holiday in a caravan in Scotland: it was rainy and windy, so we stayed inside the caravan, playing cards happily as a family. It wasn't what we planned, but the sense of togetherness was actually heightened by the fact we were united together in close proximity by the weather.

CHOOSING YOUR DESTINATION

There are many options when it comes to holidays, and making choices for what to do can be a challenge in itself: it is not easy to be able to please everyone. Usually, we have to choose to stay at home or go away.

Staying at home is safe and affordable, but home can also be a place where everyday tasks and habits can manifest, like housecleaning, work, or arranging kids to attend holiday clubs. It requires creativity to change the mundane location into a holiday full of contentment and enjoyment. Maybe designate areas of the house to be used differently, or outlaw your usual activities and do different ones. In this way you can change the humdrum home into a place of play and happy holiday. Enjoy the familiarity, but shake things up a bit as well. There's nothing like a touch of novelty to bring your awareness into the present moment.

Setting off to holiday in a brand new location brings a multitude of possibilities. There are a whole host of things to navigate from the moment you leave the house.

You may like adventurous backpacking off the beaten path, or a packaged holiday; whatever you prefer, you will be dealing with a lot of changes, both in your external surroundings and your internal responses. Travelling with children can be eye-opening and life-enhancing as we experience interesting new people, places, different cultures. However, we also have to face the difficulties of unfamiliar climates, languages, customs, ways of being and behaving, including different attitudes to children, and the practicalities of making sure our kids' needs are still met. You're likely to feel frazzled some of the time, but take a moment where you can to be mindful and re-centre yourself. In the end, how you approach the journey matters most of all, and if you can keep your children feeling loved and attended to, the rest doesn't matter so much.

Being
Creative
Together

Giving yourself time to be creative can be a beautiful way of becoming mindful. Some people also find it easier and more beneficial than trying to be still and silent, as in a formal sitting meditation practice; if that sounds like you, then go with what works. It can be difficult for fathers to create time for creativity outside of specific contexts such as work or house projects, particularly in the first few years when there are so many other pressing needs. But many men enjoy the sense of being focused on a project and the energy of fresh ideas, so when the kids are old enough, do try and clear time for it. Think of it this way: children are rarely quiet and still enough for regular meditation, so this may be one of your best chances to be mindful together with them.

BEING A MAKER

In a world that sometimes disempowers us all, giving your imagination free rein can enliven you to rise like a phoenix, to be fully alive and responsive in the rest of your life. Even little acts of creativity, like a short poem or a dance across the living room with your child, can help make a positive difference to your day, and making regular time for creativity will have an even stronger effect: it creates a positive habit of attention and intention, a free-flowing current in your lifestream.

Children are naturally inventive, and by being involved in that, you share a magical part of their world where they feel powerful, potent and full of possibility. The capacity for children to create the small things also helps them find confidence in their ability to create their whole lives.

We can encourage them to be resourceful and present by expressing interest in their ideas, helping them to explore their thoughts and express themselves clearly. If they are unsure of what to do next or how to do something, ask them open questions: what would they like to do next? What would be a fun method to try? This is a good way to support them, but it's actually a good way to re-teach yourself as well; after all, those are helpful questions to ask yourself when you're facing your own everyday challenges.

What art forms would you and your child both enjoy? Can you write and perform a song together? Create a poem? A painting? A play? The outcome doesn't matter: it's the process that counts most, and we may need to lower our desires and expectations of the final result. Your shared masterpiece may not be ready for an art gallery or a stage, but the bond you create with your child may outlast it by decades. (Many parents do, though, keep drawings and paintings by their children for a long time, and there's no reason not to do that too.)

BEING FREE TOGETHER

One creative activity my daughter and I both love is painting, and doing it together creates a free space for our imaginations to play. We take turns creating colourful brush-marks and patterns, responding to what the other person has done, and we see where it goes. Something new and unexpected emerges before our eyes in a delightful process of discovery.

We also dance, creating magical moments of mindfulness, playfully moving through time and space together with endless blends of movements. Some are unique free-form improvisation and others are learned from dance classes, gymnastics, martial arts, street dance, ballet . . . together, we are without limits. And we're also safe to be ridiculous: falling, bumping into things and nearly knocking over furniture is part of the fun. When I see my daughter full of delight, I become delighted.

There's the pleasure of what we do, such as painting or dancing, but there are other benefits to be had as well. Mindfulness allows us to see if we have particular habits in what we make or how we approach the making process, as well as how we relate to our children and ourselves. Once we become aware of this, we can encourage ourselves and our children to try new things. We can also notice what fears we or our children have about being seen and judged, about risking disapproval, and start to move through these anxieties to a healthy pride in ourselves. Both good art and good life skills come out of a place where we feel free to experiment, make mistakes and laugh without shame, or to be very focused without being told not to 'take yourself so seriously'. Helping your child find their creative voice is an invaluable gift, and giving them the mindful support they need when they're young is the foundation for a joyful, self-reliant adulthood.

Devices of
Mass Distraction
& Miraculous Invention

It is easy to be inspired, or devilishly distracted, by a bright multi-coloured magical box of technological tricks which fits in the palm of your hand – or even takes up a wall. There's no point being embarrassed about this: they are designed to be seductive. They're neither bad nor good: computers and mobile devices can be used to both connect and inspire us, and to disconnect and distract us from pleasure and meaning. And they aren't going away. Technology has made huge advances in the last few decades, and our children will be able to do things in the future that we probably cannot imagine now.

Parents have never been presented with such a vast array of possibilities, the range of which may require mindful contemplation. Just as our thoughts, words or actions can create harm or good, so too can a few clicks and taps on screens and buttons. Like anything else, it is not the item itself which is the problem, but how we use it.

HOW YOU USE TECHNOLOGY

Technology use can have many effects on your wellbeing and ability to parent your children wholeheartedly. When tired or stressed, it's easy to reach towards an app to avoid doing something more energetic together. And while mindfulness is wonderful, there's no point being a perfectionist: sometimes we need a break from the intensity of providing wholesome entertainment and education for our kids, and we're lucky that there are so many positive productions these days that can be entertaining, educational and pro-social. Mindfulness includes accepting reality, and the reality is that sometimes we're tired.

However, there is also a myriad of software which, when misused, can numb our capacity to be fully aware, happy and healthy. If we leave it up to social media or the mass media to educate our children, we may miss out on opportunities to create more mindful ways of being.

The first step is to be aware of how technology affects you. You may be familiar with a multitude of devices; you may even be reading this on a hand-held tablet or a large screen rather than a physical book. How do the differences feel? Are you more switched on, or off, by technology? For instance, I tend to read a book more slowly and reflectively than a screen; how is it for you?

POSITIVE USES

Technology can be used to enhance learning experiences. There are apps to create digital photos, videos, poems, paintings, soundscapes, animations, clothing, living environments, the list goes on, and these may be a great way to play with your child. You can use a phone to add regular reminders to pause and have mindful moments in your day. An audio or video recording can support a mindfulness meditation; a podcast on fathering can give you great ideas to try. All in all, there's a lot of good stuff out there: you just need to curate what you consume so that you're using your tech time productively – whether it's to improve your parenting skills, or to give you a break from parenting so you can come back refreshed.

GOOD CONNECTIONS

Devices can also help us engage with the people we love: creating connections with family and friends across vast distances and time zones has never been easier. This is good support for any dad – it's hard to parent if you don't feel part of a loving community – and it's great for developing your mindfulness practice as well. I am always amazed at the feeling of closeness and camaraderie when I run online yoga and meditation events: people practising together and sharing the value of what they discover through mindfulness is truly inspiring.

It's incredible to think we can forge connections with hundreds of people that we may never meet in person, but share so much in common with. A whole wonderful community that is available at our fingertips.

TAKING A MINI BREAK

Mindfulness isn't about giving ourselves or others a hard time in order to get everything right when it comes to device usage, so that's not the approach I encourage. It's really just about making sure that we use our devices, instead of them using us. The best way to get some clarity on that is to make some device-free time regularly; it could be just for a few moments in the day when you switch off or silence your device so you can be more wholeheartedly attentive to yourself, your child and the world around you. Skilful use and moderation are the way to go: as with so much else about mindful parenting, it's all about balance.

Bedtime
Boundaries

Babies seem to dictate their bedtimes to us. Some
need more connection and comfort, or just don't want
to go to sleep; others are easy to put down and settle
into routines. As babies become children many fathers
find themselves in the position of having to lay down
bedtime boundaries. You may be familiar with a phrase
like this coming out of your mouth: 'You need to be
in bed by this time, so that you can . . .' (or, indeed,
the secret corollary, 'So that I can . . .'. Parents need a
rest too – and that can include needing a bit of time at
the end of the day when the children are in bed so you
can unwind, practise some self-care, and do a quieter
mindfulness meditation).

DRILL SERGEANT OR PUSHOVER

Choosing when to be flexible or firm can be a hard learning curve, and it helps to know whether you're more likely to err on the side of 'drill sergeant' or 'pushover'. You may need to stay strong, and your kids may not like you making choices that feel like a loss of freedom, but their wellbeing has to come before their immediate wishes. This is where a mindful understanding of your own feelings comes in: holding the line without being unkind can be a delicate line to walk, and the more aware you are of what's going on inside you, the better you'll be able to keep your temper, make good decisions and avoid jumping to conclusions.

FIVE MORE MINUTES, DAD?

Most children want to stay up as late as possible: they'd rather stretch the day out than get enough sleep, and adults aren't immune to this mistake either. It helps if you can gently steer their state of mind towards sleep, which is both an art and science.

You can take the rational approach: explaining the effects of sleeplessness can sometimes help persuade them. At other times, more fun approaches can work wonders. At the age of six my daughter loved being tickled before bed, which sounds counter-intuitive but somehow seemed to settle her, perhaps because it expelled restless energy, or because the pure happiness of physical playing helped tame our little tiger. The point is, we wouldn't have learned this if we'd tried to be too by-the-book: you have to be willing to experiment. Just as mindfulness involves accepting your thoughts and feelings without judgement, mindful parenting involves embracing the approach that works for you.

And, of course, bedtime may not be the only time you have to settle your child as they wake up for one reason or another, and you have to be able to be a responsive dad during the night. Take a deep breath, and mindfully accept that you have to offer a reassuring presence to soothe the soul of your restless sleeper. This too shall pass, so be there as kindly as you can.

BOUNCING OUT OF BED

Does your child bounce out of bed in the morning because they can't wait to start the day, or do they appear to be glued to the mattress? People have different times of day when they function better than others. We probably all know people who are super-alert and alive late at night (night owls) and others that are awake at the crack of dawn (early birds). And often, parents and children find their rhythms out of sync.

We all need some healthy discipline in life, including when to go to bed and when to get out of it. Motivating oneself out of bed is an art, and parents can help set an example. The most important thing is to listen to both your own needs and your child's, and find ways to respond to each other, even if it means acknowledging the muffled grumbles of your teenager every morning. Teenagers may need a seemingly endless amount of sleep which can be frustrating, so cast your mind back to when you were a teen yourself and try to recall your or a friend's need to sleep until noon. Do you remember how tired you felt all the time? How would you have preferred to be woken, and can you now empathize with your parents in that situation? Maybe both you and your child are live-wires, and perhaps that means they need more guidance on how to fully relax and fall asleep at a reasonable hour. If this is the case, you may have knowledge that can help: what helps you fall asleep when you're feeling restless? Hopefully the practices of waking up and settling down to sleep at in their teenage years will be carried on into their adult life. It will feel like a real balancing act, so keep listening and reflecting on your own experiences as well as your child's.

Timelines

Every day is finite, and every human being seems to have their own relationship to time. We travel along imaginary tracks, checking in on watches, phones and clocks to keep to the commitments we've made and make sure they happen on the right day, hours and minute. We generally communicate this system to our children so we have a frame of reference to live by: schools, colleges and activities all require the ability to be there when you're expected. But until they've got the hang of it, parents face the problem of holding their children to a concept the kids don't understand – and that can be a frustrating responsibility.

Many fathers struggle with the conflict between a kind of timeless zone of childhood, where the kids don't really see any importance in 'what time it is', and the knowledge that being on time and respecting other people's plans do actually matter. Kids also won't necessarily be able to grasp why it's 'rude' to be really late or incredibly early, since they mostly view the world from their own perspective. Our children's developing relationship with time is an ongoing process that often reveals hidden triggers from our own personal history. Perhaps your own parents were strict time-keepers, and you were raised in a strictly scheduled environment, or maybe they were just the opposite, and you wish to raise your little ones with more order and structure.

I have often found myself getting stressed by adhering to an overly tight schedule, which is strange given that I know life can be a lot more pleasurable and fun when I let myself be less rigid. And yet I know there is value in being able to do things when they need to be done, both for our own benefit and for other people's. There is also value in being able to live in the moment, let loose and have a late night to do some stargazing, meet friends, see a performance or go camping, guided by nature's own time flow of sunrise and sunset. It doesn't have to be either-or; we can move between the two.

HOW DO YOU RELATE TO TIME?

Are you always on time, always early, always late? Do you keep checking your watch, or do you think people make far too much fuss about punctuality? Being mindful of our relationship to time and learning to understand how our loved ones relate to the concept and experience of it, can help us be creative and responsive to the whole family's needs. Especially with children, this may include letting go of a conceptual time frame for a while and being in a looser, more 'timeless' time.

You can experiment with both ways of being. On a day when you don't have to do anything in particular, try not to look at any time-tracking device and feel that freedom of being outside of time. On the other hand, try doing things for a set period of time and making a game out of it with your children so it becomes fun, like a time-tracking team on a special mission together; that can build a healthy respect for timekeeping without letting it rule your family like a tyrannical king. Every child has activities they struggle to do promptly, so no doubt you'll have plenty of opportunity to reality-test how things are going.

GETTING OUT THE DOOR

Trying to get your child ready for school in the morning can be a battle of wills; some days you will win and other days you will lose. Preparing and eating breakfast, getting dressed, gathering everything that they need for the day, making sure that the clothes that you've dressed them in are clean and not covered in toothpaste – these things can make your mornings feel like a battle of wills. Sometimes I find that trying to be on their team is the better solution, the two of us racing the clock together – and when all else fails, there's always old-fashioned bribery, like, 'If we leave now you can have some play in the park later.' Some battles are worth fighting, and in the big scheme of things, others aren't that important. Being mindful and open to experimenting with lots of different methods could be the foundation for a range of solutions. You may find your mornings a lot easier if you're not fighting an unwinnable war against your child and time itself.

Stillness
& Solitude

Sitting still and giving mindful attention to yourself, even for a few minutes a day, can make a difference to your overall sense of wellbeing. Silent time, alone or with other people, can also be very pleasant. The difficulty, for a father, is finding it.

When your child is a baby, you can sometimes have moments of meditative peace and quiet when they are asleep on you, or in a pram or bed. Some children also like being still and sitting with their parents as they meditate quietly, and we can help them learn the skills of being mindful by asking them to place a hand on their belly as they breathe. It is worth a try; some children take to it naturally and enjoy it, though many children can only sustain being still for a short duration. Some children, on the other hand, are absolute dynamos and struggle to stay still for even a second. If you can entice them to sit and meditate for even a minute, or half a minute, you're still helping them. If they really can't relax without some sensory input – which is the case with some children, we're all built differently – you can add background noise, such as nature sounds or ASMR recordings. They may build up their abilities over time, as long as they feel it as a place of acceptance, not pressure. Let go of what a mindful experience 'should' be like and meet them where they're at.

As our children get older, it becomes more possible to enjoy longer periods of quiet time, both in their company and while they are at nursery, school, with family or friends, or just entertaining themselves. A lot depends on your particular child's needs, but when the quiet moments happen, you can give yourself time and space to reflect, contemplate and meditate on your life, and what you need to nourish yourself as an individual human being aside from family. This isn't selfish at all: when you return your attention to them, you will be feeling more positive, energetic and patient.

FINDING FOCUS

Many spiritual traditions encourage people to go away, whether to a solitary cabin high up in the mountains or a quiet space in an inner-city temple, or health and wellbeing centre. This may sound like aiming a bit high for a new father; for now, maybe just consider it a sign of how seriously practitioners can take the need for peace.

Doing nothing other than being and breathing can let the whole nervous system calm down. Sensing the subtle movements inside your body, the pulse of your heart, can remind you of the fluid, ever-changing nature of life within and all around you – and yet the feeling of being stable and still soothes the soul. It is a deep knowing that you don't have to totally control your body and mind: we can let our thoughts come and go as though they are clouds passing by across a blue sky.

In the early stages of mindfulness practice, it can feel like every time we have a work- or family-related thought, we have to rise up and act on it immediately. Often, with a bit of practice of thinking it through, we can realize that the so-called 'urgent thing' can wait a while, and we may even do it better once we have been quiet and mindful for a while. Some people choose to sit with a small notepad or device next to them during their practice so that they can make a quick note and won't forget the 'important thought' before they return to sensing their breathing. If that helps you settle, go ahead – just remember to switch off the device's internet connection.

MAKING TIME

The duration we can be still for, and our appreciation of its value, can develop as we learn the subtle pleasures of being fine-tuned into ourselves. You may start with a few minutes, and gradually extend it to fifteen, thirty, or more if you wish.

In the longer term, it may be possible to gradually increase the time available for yourself over the years. When your kids grow older, you are more free to take half days, whole days, weekends or week retreats. Retreats can allow a simple rhythm of life, rising with the sun, meditating, walking, reflecting, eating when the body naturally needs it, and watching the sun pass through the sky until it sets. It can be helpful to be somewhere beautiful, preferably with a view of an expanse of sky, landscape or water before you, be it a park, or area of woodland, or a view from a balcony to allow your sense of vision to expand before and after meditation, and create a spacious state of mind that sees the world as bigger than any individual problems.

Sometimes we need to remind ourselves that we are a 'human being' rather than a 'human doing'. Communicate with your family to make it clear that you are taking time to rest so that you can be resilient and present when you return. They might also want to take time out too. Go on: make some space for yourselves to be still and silent.

Friendship,
a True
Treasure

Friendship between fathers can be a real treasure, particularly in these modern times when many people feel isolated. So many conditions can separate us – distance, race, age, culture, beliefs – yet these differences can also be sources of interest and inspiration, and none of them should inhibit your innate drive to create new friendships and forge new connections.

As fathers we can feel cut off from other individuals, even in public environments that invite one-on-one connection and communication such as playgrounds and playdates. As we spend more time in social settings with our kids in these places, it's good to be open to spontaneous moments of connection with another dad. We never know who is going to walk in or out of our lives, sometimes fleetingly, sometimes to become a dear friend. We all have our own comfort levels, so it's a question of feeling out yours and expanding your awareness outwards to encompass the fathers around you. Even an exchange of pleasantries, a smile or a 'good morning' could be the small spontaneous start to a friendship or may even simply bring a smile to another's face. Think about how much you would value a friendly exchange after a rough night's sleep or a bad day. Passing along the good intention that you feel for others in any way you can will give you a chance to spark a new friendship and brighten your life with a new connection.

TAKING OPPORTUNITIES

One day, a few years ago I took my daughter to a park to play. After a while I saw a guy who had a daughter of a similar age to mine, so I thought I would be friendly and say hello. We greeted each other, and had a nice conversation, while the kids played together on swings. He and his daughter were both friendly, so we exchanged contact details and started arranging playdates. We now spend some time together at many weekends and our families are good friends. Through knowing them, we also became connected to a lovely community of people with children of similar ages. I sometimes reflect on how much we might have missed out on if we hadn't made the effort to connect.

TAKING RISKS

A friend of mine made a card for me many years ago with a painting of a boat and some writing which was something like this:

'A "friend ship" is a vessel which helps you navigate the sea of life.'

When it comes to meeting new people, there is always an element of going into the unknown, a going out of our own little 'self-ship' with the potentiality of creating a 'friend-ship' which is a bigger vessel than the sum of its parts, carrying a cargo of knowledge and culture we can share with each other. It's not always easy to connect with people: we may not be the sort of person to reach out, or we may create thoughts like 'They don't look interested, or interesting', or 'They won't like me'. Some of these thoughts may date back to when we were first playing in playgrounds as children ourselves – but often with a little self-reflection we can challenge them. They are just thoughts, and perhaps we don't need to hang on to them any more. Ultimately, we have nothing to lose other than an old idea or view of ourselves or another person. And we may be able to create something beautiful and true: fantastic new friendships for your child and for you too.

When we have this awareness of ourselves, we can then become more aware of the other person as we reach out to connect with them. Though we can never know what will happen, more often than not we find that a little courage and understanding will breach the gap between your 'self-ship' and theirs, allowing you both to share a little knowledge and ultimately grow from the experience.

The potential for friendship is present wherever there are people, and of course, being in places with like-minded people may help you to meet others who are compatible with you. I really like the spontaneous meetings in unlikely places that flourish into friendships, though. Whether it's by the school gate or at the supermarket, at the park or at a sports game, don't let pre-conceived ideas discourage you: if you're mindful of the presence of other people, and the goodness within the human heart, you may find more than you expected.

Community & Communication

Whether we like it or not, we need other human beings. What we think of as community will vary; what we like or dislike about it will depend on our own histories. Personally, I feel a deep need to know, and be known by, other human beings, and I don't believe that I am alone in that need. I have been involved in different groups over the years focused around art, work, yoga, Buddhism and self-development, each with their own philosophies and values. I appreciate and learn different qualities being involved with each of them.

Men often gather around a shared activity or interest. The good thing about having children is that fatherhood itself can be a shared activity: we are often brought together by a need to socialize our children, or even by chance. Trips to parks, playgrounds, clubs or family gatherings are all places to bond with other dads.

A HEALTHY MIND

Mental health issues have been an increasing problem for men. The pressure to succeed, and to base your sense of identity in what you achieve in the world, is all around us, and the harm this does is not small: suicide rates amongst men aged between eighteen and fifty-nine have been at an all-time high in recent years.

Men need to be able to talk about difficulties in life, both admitting them privately to ourselves and discussing them with trusted friends, instead of 'keeping a lid' on our emotions. Mindfulness helps us learn to be aware of how we are and what we need, and this is the foundation of going out into our community and finding ways to get those needs met. Seeing to our own emotional nourishment through a community of like-minded people who are experiencing similar trials and tribulations will make us less likely to stifle our feelings, and can go a very long way towards preventing a build-up of negative thoughts and stress that may be unintentionally passed on to the friends and family around us.

COMPASSIONATE WITNESSES

Fathering can be lonely without regular interaction with other men who recognize you. Being witnessed, heard and understood by men who share your experiences of sleepless nights; the ups and downs of milestones at every age; kids' education at nursery, school or university; and the complexities of your relationship with your children, is very affirming. It goes beyond a simple sharing of the fact of having created a child: we can share what it means, in a deep sense, to be human.

Many modern cultures have an image of a 'real man': individual, standing alone like an island, able to take on and conquer the world. Strength and self-reliance are good things, but they need to be counterbalanced by the fact that we are also social creatures. We are defined as much by our interdependent relationships as our ability to be independent. Developing an ability to communicate honestly and heartfully is invaluable. Often men have been encouraged to hide emotion, incorrectly taught that it's feminine or weak to have feelings – but modern research is revealing that being in tune with your more sensitive side and feeling free to be honest about it is good for you. If you make the first step to discuss more sensitive topics with your group, they may feel more inclined to open up about their own troubles. This way, everyone can experience and share in mutual feelings, share tips or just feel that they are being heard. With courage and mindfulness towards others, we can create a level ground where men can support and be supported by one another.

CELEBRATIONS

Male comradeship isn't all about sharing the sad stuff. Consider, for instance, sharing food: it's both a basic survival need and a traditional way of coming together.

Children's birthday parties and other communal celebrations are also a regular part of life, so get the most out of them: they're a great way of gathering.

I have had the pleasure of being involved in a local community who love socializing over food and drink while talking about what's happening in their life. The conversation ranges from recent trials and tribulations of parenting, to what their child is learning and enjoying, to stressful hospital visits and all that brings – the good and the bad that make up the stuff of life. The old phrase 'A problem shared is a problem halved' comes to mind. I think many of us feel a sense of solidarity in being held in heart and mind by other people.

Find a community of people you like and love, or, if necessary, create one. There is, perhaps, no greater gift than the giving and receiving of friendship.

Family Ancestry

Whether you have met every member of your family, live close to or far from your relatives, or your relations live on only in photographs and your memory, you are always part of an ancestral line. We may not know what your forebears did or how they lived, but patterns of thought, speech and action can be inherited unconsciously. Because of it, if you do have access to your biological family, it can be helpful to understand them so you can learn what good traits you want to honour, and what unhelpful habits you want to let go. Of course, your family may not be the people you are related to biologically; if you are adopted, the choice to look into your family of origin is deeply personal and best decided upon mindfully – but you will still have inherited a lot of assumptions and customs from your adopted forebears, so it's useful to have an insight into them whether you're related by blood or not.

WHEN I WAS YOUNG . . .

It is all too easy to judge our parents, grandparents, and great-grandparents before them, but it's important to remember that we may never know and totally understand the living conditions they went through. Much has changed in our world, both in material conditions and in cultural assumptions and access to information; when you look at your forebears, try to do it with an open mind. Every generation lives through significant global events, and understanding your family, the historical cultural conditioning, as well as environmental and economical history can help us know and take responsibility for our part in the global village. Depending on their age, our parents may not have had access to the amount of information we now have available at our fingertips via the internet. They couldn't get instant answers to their questions, and they won't have had a favourite TV show downloaded on their phone to entertain you as an impatient infant in the car.

Of course, we don't have to excuse it if our parents, or theirs, were outright cruel. Understanding that everyone faces their own challenges doesn't mean we have to put up with degrading treatment; you deserved to be treated well, and if you weren't, mindfulness isn't about writing that experience off. If your family includes a history of abuse, you have a particular challenge to face; in your situation, understanding someone's circumstances may simply be a case of recognizing how they came to mistreat you or others, and using that insight to strengthen your resolution to be stronger and kinder than they were. Take care of your own feelings and be gentle with yourself: that is how you learn to be gentle with others. Whether your family was warm and safe or harsh and painful, deep transformation takes time and effort, and mindfulness is a key part of that process. The ability to inwardly inquire, reflect, and engage in being honest with yourself and your family is powerful. It's about making the active choice to be a positive influence in the family you have now.

THE ANCESTOR AS INDIVIDUAL

I don't know a lot about my family, other than some stories handed down by my father and mother. As in all families, there are tales of facing the difficult aspects of life – career choices, wars, illnesses – as well as happier memories, such as holidays.

I know when I first started to become aware of aspects of my father's personality I didn't always find comfortable, like his preoccupation with punctuality, his insistence on doing things in particular ways, his emphasis on being tidy, learning to earn a living, planning ahead, and focus on mortgages and pensions. I wanted to push them, or him, away, until I realized the difficulties he had faced himself. Now I wish I had listened more fully when I was younger. We live and learn!

I remember not understanding, as a teenager, why my father appeared stressed at times. I now know that he had been commuting daily for years, working in a very responsible role to help support his family (alongside my mother, who was working equally hard in different ways). I now feel grateful for all the efforts they made, and it was only really by becoming a father myself, with some similar responsibilities and roles, that I began to feel empathy, and consciously accepted and loved him more fully. He, like many of us, was doing the best he possibly could.

As long as you can live your life with a loving awareness, and create an intention to show appreciation and gratitude where possible, and forgiveness where necessary (for you or for them), there is possibility of learning from the past to be fully present, now and in the future.

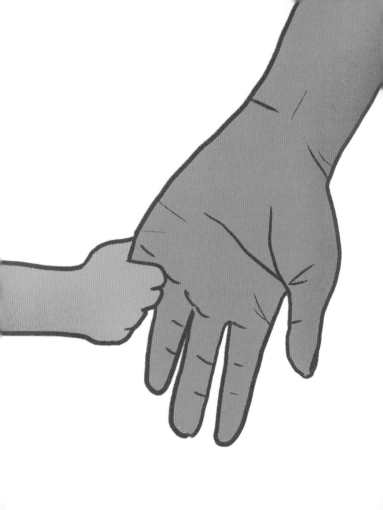

A Legacy
of Love

What legacy will you leave behind for your child or children? Your every thought, word and action can become a source of nourishment and inspiration for other actions of love and awareness inside them. Of course we have to put bread on the table, as the saying goes, but by creating mindful moments of love, you are also feeding their characters, their hearts and souls. If we give them the time, attention and love that they need and deserve now, they will carry that love into the future. As they mature, your fathering today, tomorrow, and in the years ahead will nourish their ability to be well and happily engaged in life.

PAST, PRESENT AND FUTURE

Often, when mindfulness is taught, the emphasis is primarily on being present now. Yes, we absolutely need to be aware in the moment; however, if we are not aware of how our past habits are influencing us, we are missing opportunities for transformation. There is value in thinking ahead to the future, to affect how we think and behave in the present. Obviously, it is unhelpful if we are continually caught up in looking ahead, but perhaps we can create a balanced approach of reflecting back, and imagining forwards, to create what is helpful here and now. Thinking about what you, your child and your family need in five, ten or thirty years could make a difference to you all.

WHAT WILL YOUR CHILD REMEMBER?

I imagine that you would rather be remembered as a loving parent who gave your son or daughter all they needed to grow in confidence and become who they desired to be. What can you do now to nurture those beautiful qualities in them that will become a true asset to their personality and character? How can you parent in service to what they, and possibly the world, may need when they are adults? What are their particular interests, skills or talents that, given attention and kind encouragement, may become a wonderful positive source of self-esteem, and a force for good in the world?

You can never completely know who your child will become, and of course, it is ultimately up to them. Part of our responsibility as parents is recognizing that we do have some influence, and also that there is no way we can control everything.

CHOOSING AND LETTING GO

To some extent, you can choose to contribute to what your own legacy will be. It may be more giving finances, time or energy, or supporting physical, mental and emotional qualities. Every father-child relationship is different. At the end of the day we don't know how our child is going to remember us. You may be remembered for things you did, but some of the influence you have in shaping your child's character will also be down to what you didn't do. This may be particularly true in the teen years, when they are comparing their parents to other people's and evaluating what they have or don't have, both materially and emotionally.

Whether or not they find such differences easy to accept will depend a lot on their own disposition as well as your parenting – and, of course, what you were and weren't able to provide for them along the way. But sharing values such as the ability to accept life as it is can go beyond any specific phase, context or lifestyle, and is fundamentally supportive to your child's psyche. Passing along a mindful acceptance of your own lives, not resenting the situation of others, not tallying up the material possessions others have compared to you and living in the present: all of this will serve to increase your and your family's happiness now and in the distant future.

Personally, I am still learning from my father, and will continue to through my life. I am grateful to have received a variety of his qualities such as his strong work ethic, commitment to standing by what you believe in, his loyalty, and his understanding of the value of loving your family. The legacy you leave your children may be different from what you might imagine, and there's no way you can fully determine what they think and feel about you. All you can do is give them as much positive love and attention as you can, and hope some of that gets stored in their memory banks as they mature. If that happens, they will remember their time with you as a legacy of love.

A Father's
Love Continues

As fathers, we have the opportunity, the responsibility, and hopefully the joyful pleasure, of creating a journey of loving awareness for ourselves and our family. While making a child often comes partly from a desire for the personal pleasure of making love with the child's mother, our caring can also expand and become less self-focused, turning our regard to our partner, children, communities, and to the world that we inhabit. We can offer the paternal qualities developed in fatherhood to the wider context of society.

Wherever you are in your journey of being a father, the love you create will continue in the heart and mind of your child. My wish for you is that they grow into a human being full of beautiful qualities, a branch of your family tree and the forest of life on this planet – and, if they have children, hopefully they too will continue the process of sharing the gifts of loving attention you have given them over the years.

PAUSING TO BE PRESENT

I would like to invite you to pause and take a moment to be present now, sensing how your body feels. Sense your spine, your legs, your feet, your arms and hands, your head and face. Feel the air around you, moving in and out of your body as you breathe: place a hand on your stomach if that helps you feel your breath move in and out. Allow your body and mind to rest as much as you can for a few minutes, including holding an awareness of your thoughts and feelings.

Then, when you feel ready, recollect an experience (or a few) you have had as a father that brought you joy and pleasure. Notice what that feels like: savour it, soak it up and appreciate it for a few moments until you feel saturated. Then, after a little while, slowly let that experience dissolve away, and return to being aware of your body and breathing for a few moments.

When you feel ready, recollect an experience as a father that has been challenging or a little bit difficult; nothing too heavy – don't overwhelm yourself. Choose something that you feel you have grown from, or that has taught you something about yourself, your child, or life itself. Notice how that feels, physically, mentally and emotionally, and how it changes your sense of yourself. Then gradually return to awareness of your breathing and rest for a few moments.

The first recollection may have felt lighter and warmer emotionally, and the second one probably a bit heavier. Now send your thoughts forwards and outwards to the future, and also recollect your past and ancestry, connecting to your sense of what is behind you. Listen to how you feel during this journey along your timeline: explore the joyous moments, the worries, the fears and the moments of love and kindness that call to you.

These are four aspects and directions of fathering: up and down, forwards and backwards – all important and real. Mindfulness can help us move towards equanimity, so we can experience all facets more equally and fully, ultimately moving in the direction of accepting life as it is.

MAKING THE MOMENTS

Give yourself time on a regular basis to tune in with how you are feeling. It will help you be a father who can give attention to his children and family in a loving, sustainable way. If we can make efforts to look after our internal climate and create a wealth of positive intentions in our own hearts and minds, we can create a loving, mindful life for our child, helping them become an adult who feels free and happy to create the life they want to live.

I hope the process of reading this book has been helpful for you, and that there have been a few good light-bulb moments, or at least a few thoughts that will inspire continued exploration of mindfulness. If you are interested, there are many resources available which can help you learn in more depth; mindfulness is growing in popularity as people open up to its benefits, and a quick internet search will find you a wealth of useful sites and suggestions.

If nothing else, I hope I have helped you gain some understanding that mindfulness is not about escaping life, but about engaging with it. You begin with the inner world of your body, thoughts and feelings, but you balance this with your sense of the world around you, your children, your home, and what you do in the world. In this way, you can learn to be present with whatever is in your experience. We are travelling along a journey of loving awareness, and the wheels of life roll on. I hope you enjoy your journey. May you and your family be well, may you be happy, and may you be at peace.

ACKNOWLEDGEMENTS

With thanks to friends and teachers: Padmavaira, Surata, Triratna Buddhist Order and Mark Walsh. Wendy Ann Greenhalgh, Riga Forbes (for suggesting I write this book), Peirs Moore Ede, Piergiullo Poli, for believing in me and reminding me of the early phases of fathering.

In remembrance of Antonia Laurenti Baule and Nick Diggins, who passed away during the writing of this book. Your memories will live on in the hearts of many. May you be at peace.

DEDICATION

To my parents, Anne and Anthony Griffiths: thank you for loving me through my life. To Tania and Chris for being great examples, and my nephews. My precious family: Silvia, my partner, and Francesca, my fun-loving daughter. Renato and Antonia Laurenti, for bringing Silvia into the world and helping her along the way.
Karunavira, Dharmavasita, Indrabodhi and Mokshini, for inspiring me to parent mindfully. And my fellow fathers: Alastair, Siggi, Leo, Gabriel, Carlos, Mark, Sudaka and Ketuhridaya.